MW01256671

99 Things a Student Needs to Learn before Graduating from High School

Mary Stefano

ISBN: 146369928X
ISBN 13: 9781463699284

This book is dedicated to my students and colleagues in education.

Education is a journey to the answer.

Mark Twain said,
"When I was a boy of fourteen, my father
was so ignorant I could hardly stand to have
the old man around. But when I got to be
twenty-one, I was astonished at how much
the old man had learned in seven years."

Introduction

—⁓—

Having taught adolescents for thirty-four years, I can affirm that many who graduate or spend time with me in the classroom have asked questions about the basics of education and human development that school or family life had not taught them. Sometimes we teach the discipline, and sometimes we teach LIFE. To that end, I explained to the best of my ability the answers, or I sought the answers with them. Some of these students asked me point-blank, "Why don't they teach this in high school?" My reply was, "School will not teach you all you need to know."

We need to be lifelong learners and have a thirst for knowledge that will always have us seeking answers. This book contains some of the basics I came up with as I experienced my students' lack of knowledge through my career as an educator; what society may call common sense turns out not to be so common. I have attempted to glean from the American public what has been lost in translation for our younger generations.

One thing remains true through all the technology and social media: good etiquette will always be a foundation of human interaction. We cannot expect school systems or families to teach everything that one needs to live a full life. We need to fill in the gaps with a desire for knowledge so great that it never ends, a desire to consistently improve our existence by learning to do the simple things in life with knowledge and grace.

These 99 things are *all* important. In no particular order, I have divided the topics into three sections: correspondence and communication, verbal and written; social etiquette and personal care; and daily living and education.

Part One

Correspondence and Communication, Verbal and Written

—⁓—

Use each interaction to be the best, most powerful version of yourself. —Marianne Williamson

1

Learn how to manage your time and how to monitor it. **Learn how to respect others' time.** The older you get, the more time is valued. Not that time isn't important when you're young, but there is an exponential value on it as we get older, probably because so many things pull our personal time from us: careers, family life, extended families, and home chores. Learning a skill to make the best use of time when you are young develops a pattern that you can take into any situation and be an effective time manager. When doing your homework or writing a term paper, stick with it; get it done! When at the library researching, get it done, and then start to read other things. Immediacy and task completion will give you a great sense of peace and freedom. Learn to arrive a bit early and plan ahead. No one will chastise you if you are early, but being late is always a negative. If you make this a pattern, you will eliminate an existence of eternal panic. Being fashionably late is not fashionable!

2

Learn how to invite guests and host them at your home or in public. Mention the type of affair it is and what time to arrive, and wait until they ask if they can bring something before dictating. You may wish to have a standard response: "Please bring nothing except for some good conversation." (That's what I like to say!) Remember to give directions to your home if they haven't been there before.

3

Learn how to give a speech. At a wedding, in a business meeting. at the Boy Scout troop meeting, or in your yoga class, you may need to address a group of people. State the reason you are speaking, what you have to say about it, and a summary. Learn how to stand still, smile, and make good eye contact with a small or large audience.

4

Learn how to initiate and carry on a conversation. Also know when not to talk. Know how to politely ask for information and how to actively listen. We build our relationships, both professional and personal, on conversations and communication. The best friends you will have are those who think you're a good listener.

5

Learn how to verbally thank someone and receive thanks graciously. Be authentic in your gratitude and allow your words to describe your feelings. "Thank you so much for the lovely birthday gift. Turning thirty is so much more special with this lovely watercolor painting, especially done by someone whom I admire so much. It will be placed in a special location in my new home, and I will think of you and our friendship when I look at it. Thank you once again ever so much." Showing heartfelt gratitude and how you will be using the gift are important.

6

Learn how to pause, listen, reflect, respond, and respectfully disagree in a conversation. Rhythm in conversation is absent in e-mails or in texts. Learning to speak "face-to-face" is an art. The rhythm, pauses, and knowledge about when to listen and think about what was said are important for good conversation. Allowing others time to respond and allowing them to gather their thoughts are also vital for the continuance of a good conversation. It is better for you not to get a chance to say everything rather than to abbreviate someone else's thought. Conversations should not be a speech. Disagreeing is also an art. It is important to disagree with the point of conversation and not with the person.

7

L **earn how to ask questions during conversation to elicit information.** Quite simply, in order to ask good questions, one must listen well. Keeping on topic with questions is important. If a change of subject is provoked by your question, a pardon is in order. "Excuse me for changing the subject, but I want to ask you this question."

8

Learn the proper way to reply to either a verbal or formal written invitation. The favor of your reply, or RSVP, may be included in formal and informal invitations: "RSVP by Dec. 25, 2014." This is the cutoff date for responses. Always RSVP by this date, if not sooner. It is considered rude to leave RSVPs to the last minute. Underneath the deadline, there may be an item looking like this: "M_____." Here, you will simply need to fill out your title according to your gender. For example: Mr. Bob Smith or Mrs. Susan Jones. There will be the option of accepting or declining. Sometimes there is simply an empty space next to "Will attend," where you may place a checkmark. Other times, it may look like this: "__Accepts with pleasure __Declines with regrets." In this instance, simply check the appropriate blank. You may also leave a brief explanation or a note of congratulations. Once the card is properly filled out, mail it back to the sender. A separate envelope is often included with the RSVP card. If you receive a blank RSVP card, simply mimic the template used in standard RSVP cards. State your name in the third person, whether you will attend, and include the date of the event. Remember to use formal wording.

9

Learn how to leave a phone message and return a telephone call. When leaving a message, include your first and last name, time of your call, reason for calling, and when would be a good time to return your call. Someone who lives with the person you are calling may be writing down your message and delivering it to the person you were trying to reach. Be brief!

10

Learn how to take good notes. School is not the only time you will have to write thoughts down to remember them later. Business meetings, clubs you may join, committees you will be on, and things you want to remember to do around your home are all practical examples of instances when it will be advantageous to be an organized note taker.

11

Learn how to write in cursive and in print, even if your teachers didn't teach it. It is out there in the world. Know how to write with penmanship good enough for most anyone to read.

12

Learn how to alphabetize. It is important to learn the alphabet in order to find and organize items. For example, you may be writing a Christmas card list or organizing a list of last names for the residents in a condo association. You may be a teacher like me and alphabetize names in classes. You will not only find times you need to put lists in alphabetical order, but things out in the world like phone books, lists of hotels, books, songs on iTunes, organizations, etc. are alphabetized. You need to find *Mc* after *M* and *Y* after *X*.

13

Learn what constitutes a complete sentence and what constitutes an incomplete sentence. Be able to write a paragraph and convey your idea in a single thought. Know how to write a friendly letter, a thank-you note, and a congratulatory greeting. Know how to write a formal letter, such as a cover letter or other business correspondence. Know the proper time frame for letters to be sent.

14

Learn how to address an envelope, both written out and typed. In the upper left-hand corner should be your return address, including on line one, your first and last name; line two, street number and street name; line three, city and two-letter state abbreviation, separated by a comma. You should also include your own zip code on this line. In the center of the envelope, begin with the addressee's first and last name, and complete the address in the same manner as the return address, and be sure to include the zip code at the end of line three. In the upper right-hand corner, place a stamp for the proper postage.

15

Learn how to fold a business letter and insert it in an envelope correctly. Also know how to mail larger documents and forms that shouldn't be folded. Bring the sheet of 8.5″ × 11″ letterhead up to the top third of the letter and then fold down the top third. Place the letter in the envelope with the open flap toward the opening. Some mailings cannot be folded with a nice crease. This is the time to place the entire open letter in an accommodating envelope.

16

Learn your home phone number, cell phone number, and the numbers of significant members of your family without having to look them up on a device. Here's a good example of a time when this knowledge is imperative: You and your friend are boating for the day. You have decided to change the departure time and thus the arrival time back home. Just as you pull your cell phone out of your pocket, it sails into the lake. You must use your friend's phone to call your parents so they know your change in plans and to inform them that your phone is at the bottom of the lake. They may or may not be home, so the succession of contacts needs to be in your memory without the data you can no longer retrieve.

17

Learn the process to get a job. **Learn how to write a résumé.** Learn how to fill out an application, have a successful interview, and get a job. This may sound like a daunting task; however, seek ways to sell your best talents to an interviewer and write about them on an application. There are many styles of résumés. There are also services to help you write a résumé. It is wise to have others read your résumé for style and content. Ask the advice of one who knows and be willing to pay for the service. It is a great investment. Interview coaching is also worth the investment. At the very least, sit in a chair in front of a full-length mirror and talk about your professional life and your hobbies. Ask someone you trust and respect to give you advice while you speak.

18

Learn how to fill in an application. Use an ink pen and read the entire application before you begin writing. Think in your head where you want to include the information before writing. Often you will fill in an application at the establishment, so bring a file with names, addresses, phone numbers, and e-mail addresses of people you can list for recommendations. In each space, think before you begin to write in regard to how much space is available for each item. The application, your neatness, handwriting, and grammar make the first impression.

19

Learn how to write a cover letter. Using the different styles found on many online sources, include your complete address, phone number, and e-mail address. If you have a Twitter or LinkedIn account, it is good to give the company multiple ways to contact you. Include the complete address of the company and, if applicable, the name of the person you are writing to, the date, and a well-written letter including an introduction, a body, and a conclusion. Tell why you are writing, how you heard about the company, and what your goal is (an interview, a meeting, etc.).

Part Two
Social Etiquette and
Personal Care

—ɯ—

*Etiquette is the science of living. It embraces
everything. It is ethics. It is honor. —Emily Post*

20

Learn how to start a new friendship. Learn how to initiate good conversation by asking questions. You may have a college roommate who comes from a different state and a different religious background. Learn to ask about someone without sounding nosy. "Tell me about yourself" is a good beginning. If you are curious about a tradition, a good initial comment is, "I would like to know more about..." When I moved to a new city, I of course missed my friends that I left behind. Even though we keep in contact to this day, new friends are always fun to make.

21

Learn how to deal with children. Even though you may not have your own children at this point, learn how to deal with children at certain ages. What does a two-year-old like to do, what can a five-year-old do, a seven-year-old, etc. Knowing basic childhood development stages can engage you in a population that can bring great joy!

22

Learn how to select an appropriate hostess gift. When someone has asked you not to bring anything, a hostess gift is still in order. Flowers or a tea towel or a box of nuts or chocolates makes a nice presentation. If you are more intimate with the host—a relative or close friend—select something he or she enjoys. I know a friend who loves to entertain, so I made her a simple apron and stamped an image on the front. She loved it. A hostess gift is a thank-you for taking the time to make a meal and share it with the guest.

23

earn proper dress for informal and formal affairs and how to ask about a dress code if the event does not dictate a preference. If assuming you know the dress code leaves you uncomfortable, asking the event coordinator or the host or hostess will remove all doubt. The invitation style may hint at proper attire (e.g., for the barbecue-style invite, Bermuda shorts and T-shirts; for the engraved invitation on fine paper invite, after-five attire). When planning your wedding, birthday party, going-away party, or other affair, you can always indicate dress.

24

Learn proper wedding attire. Pardon the assumption that you will get married someday, but you may want to keep this in memory for that important occasion. Wedding attire that used to mean formal dress for men and women holds a wild card in the fashion faux pas category. Style and desire precede etiquette and tradition many times. Specific wedding attire is relegated for times of day as well. Tuxedos have their own etiquette; 6:00 p.m. is the dividing time for certain styles of tuxedos and cocktail dresses. Consulting websites or etiquette books for all the variations is advised.

25

earn how to respectfully talk and listen to older people and how to treat them without being patronizing. Someone older than you has wisdom and experiences that you can learn from. Learn to ask interesting questions of their age group. Use what happened in history to initiate those questions.

26

Learn who opens the door for whom. The younger opens the door for the older person. The man opens the door for the woman. One opens a door for the other with packages, and the same is true for all in revolving doors. There is a trend for men to not open doors for women and women to open doors for men, but if we return to tradition, there are rare instances in which it would be unacceptable.

27

Learn how to make formal and casual introductions. Know how to introduce an adult to an adolescent and vice versa. Introductions are similar to opening doors. Introduce the younger to the adult. "Dad, I would like to introduce my friend Sally to you. Sally, this is my father." Or, "Mr. Smith, this is Bob Jones. Bob, Mr. Smith."

28

Learn when to ask for help. There are times when we need the aid of a friend in making something in the kitchen or in a workshop, on the job, or driving from point A to point B. We need to respectfully ask if someone would take some time to help.

29

Learn how to receive criticism and how to give constructive criticism. Being critiqued is part of every job, every class, and every relationship. It is how we grow. It is important to hear the criticism with an open mind. Refrain from reacting with your first emotions of anger or disagreement or agreement. Let the criticism sink in and reply with calmness. Always thank someone for the criticism. They obviously care enough about you to have thought about it.

30

Learn how to deal with peer pressure. Peer pressure is a hot topic in many high schools, but each person needs to develop a system to deal with others who encourage behavior that may not be acceptable. Learn to say no politely and firmly. Protect yourself, your time, and your health by filling your moments with things you find healthy and enriching.

31

L earn how to pay your respects when someone has died. Learn how to attend the funeral and visit the family either at a funeral home or in their home, depending on their custom. Sending a sympathy card or flowers to the immediate family is a kind and welcoming gesture. Sometimes a visit is appropriate as well.

32

Know how to use silverware, how to set the table, and the proper table etiquette for dining at home or in public.

- ❖ Let your guest order first.
- ❖ Do not place your cell phone, keys, or purse on the table.
- ❖ Dress nicely.
- ❖ Don't sample others' foods.
- ❖ Place your utensils in the dish when finished.
- ❖ Wipe your fingers and mouth often with your napkin.
- ❖ Cut one piece of meat or fish at a time on your plate and eat it before cutting the next one.
- ❖ Butter bread on your plate, never in midair.
- ❖ Look into (not over) the cup or glass when drinking.
- ❖ Sit up straight, and keep your arms (including elbows) off the table.

33

Learn the courses of a formal meal: what is eaten first, second, and last. (Soup, salad, entrée, and dessert are the order usually used. In some cultures salad may be served after the entrée.) Know which cutlery is used for each course and how to set the table properly for a formal meal. (Cutlery is placed next to the plate with forks on the left and knife and spoon on the right. Forks are used from outside in. Sometimes a knife is replaced with a fish knife. The spoon can sometimes be placed above the plate for dessert purposes.) Learn how to talk during a meal. Keep the conversation light and interesting. Compliment the chef on the food prepared for you.

34

Learn CPR. Health centers, community education programs, and local fire and police departments may offer courses in CPR. It is important to seek out this education because it can save a life.

35

Learn how to cut your nails and maintain proper nail and hand hygiene. In some professions, your hands are visible and part of the work you will do. Even if your hands are not, proper hygiene includes your hands. It is important to have clean hands that have healthy, well-manicured nails. Keep the fashion colors and embellishments for social occasions and remain neutral in color and style for the workplace.

36

Learn the proper way to shave your legs or face. There are many Internet sites that teach the proper way to shave, and there are various creams to use for special skin types. Like hand hygiene, proper skin and body hygiene are good to practice.

37

Learn how to wash your hair and someone else's hair. This may sound odd, but I had to take care of my parents when they were sick and needed to wash their hair. You may have to care for someone who is ill or maybe has broken a foot and cannot shower. Learning to wash someone else's hair is a good thing!

38

Learn how to take up only one seat on a bus, train, tram, or airplane. When sitting in a public transportation seat, put your bag either on your lap or between your feet on the floor. For longer distances like on an airplane, stow one bag under the seat in front of you or in the overhead compartment. Your luggage or bags should not limit the next passenger's comfort and space.

39

earn that you should get up so someone older can sit down on any public transportation, in medical and business offices, and at social gatherings. When you are seated and someone is in your presence that is older, it is traditional and also very kind to offer your seat to that person.

40

Learn how to hang up your cell phone, iPod, or other device and interact with the cashier (or other people around you). Being on your tech device may seem like a natural part of your day and the way you communicate. But staring at a text, listening to music, or checking social media and e-mails cuts off the connection with those around you. It is rude to prefer what can wait on your device and avoid the human interaction at a given moment. Learn to hang it up and talk with others. It is a civilized human being's characteristic to communicate with each other. Look the other person in the eye; listen to what he or she says, and respond.

41

Learn when to greet someone with a handshake and/or a hug or kiss. The handshake should be firm but not crushing. The person in higher position or authority or age should initiate the greeting. Look the person in the eye when shaking hands. Offer a greeting before and during the handshake. The right hand is used for handshakes unless there is a reason to use the left. Keep the left hand visible and unclenched. If you are familiar with the person, you may use your left hand to cup the other person's arm or hand. Hugs and kisses are for intimate relationships: relatives and close friends.

42

Learn how to clean up after yourself. Whether as a roommate in college or in an apartment or visiting a relative or a friend, you need to know that the bathroom and bedroom should look as nice if not better than before you arrived. If staying overnight, it is nice to bring the bed and bath linens into the laundry room prior to leaving. If the host asks you to leave them in the rooms, fold them and place the bed linens on the corner of the bed and the towels on the sink.

43

Learn about food groups and how much of each is recommended daily. Learn how carbohydrates, proteins, fats, and grains can be incorporated into a healthy, well-balanced diet.

44

Learn how to prepare two good versions of breakfast, lunch, and dinner. Learn how to cook some egg dishes, how to make pastas and a few soups, and how to grill some meat. Learn how to prepare some healthy vegetables and salads.

45

Learn when to remove your baseball cap. It is improper to wear your baseball cap in a classroom, public office: medical or business, courtroom, religious institution: church or temple. Turning it from front to back does not define removing it. Take your hat off to show respect!

Part Three
Daily Living and Education

—ᘓ—

The only person who is educated is the one who has learned how to learn and change. —*Carl Rogers*

46

Learn how to think critically and to research information using various sources. The information age has us running to the Internet for everything from baking a cake to finding out what drugs interfere with other drugs. Use a variety of research tools including people, libraries, and trusted Internet sources to develop your opinions.

47

Learn how to make career plans and secondary plans. Know how to differentiate between hobbies and careers. Sometimes our hobbies turn into careers, and sometimes the career we initially wanted becomes the second choice. Life moves around, so be prepared.

48

Learn how to drive. Learn where you take driver's education classes and where to apply for your license. Know the costs of driving including the education, test, and vehicle costs. Owning a car includes the initial cost of the vehicle, gas, maintenance, and insurance. In some cities, it is unnecessary to own a car; public transportation is available. However, I still believe learning to drive is important because you may live in or travel to different areas of the world where driving is the best mode of transportation. Learn how to drive a stick shift and an automatic car. Also, learn how to ride a bicycle. Depending on where you live someday, one of these forms of transportation may be your only source. Having knowledge, if not expertise, is wise.

49

Learn how to replace important documents if they get misplaced: a birth certificate, a license, a social security card, and a passport. You may begin to replace these documents in the following locations. Birth certificates can be found at the hospital where you were born, at municipal offices of the town or city where you were born, or at the vital statistics office of your birth state. A driver's license can be replaced from the secretary of state pr the Department of Motor Vehicles, depending on the state in which you reside. A social security card can be replaced at secure.ssa.gov, where you can complete the necessary form. A passport may be replaced at the US Department of State (www. travel.state.gov). All or any of these documents may be needed for job and college applications. Keeping the documents in a fireproof safe is a good way to prevent misplacing them.

50

Learn how to open and maintain a bank account and checking account with a debit card. Learn how to responsibly own a credit card Learn how to balance your checkbook and how to use an ATM. Checking accounts come with debit cards that you can use for purchases with monies debited from your checking account. It is important to keep a ledger of money spent on your card even though you may see your balance after a purchase. There are fees for overdrafts (writing a check for more than the amount of money in the account). With a credit card, be aware of the interest percentage should you not pay off the credit card balance each month. It is very expensive to pay on credit. You should only do so with a reason, for example, getting something at a reduced price on a particular date that would be a better deal when figuring in the interest paid over several months of payments on the purchase. Different credit cards have different interest rates, so shop around for the best. Using an ATM safely is also important. Look around before entering information, and remember to clear your information before walking away.

51

Learn how to save money. A good rule of thumb is to save 25 to 50 percent of what you earn. If you are not paying for home expenses—mortgage, utilities, Internet, and phone—try to save more. Once you have daily living expenses, the lower percentage is a more realistic goal. It is important to not spend all of what you earn.

52

Learn how to invest your money or hire some-one who can help you. From high school or college to your first paycheck may seem like a huge step in earnings. If you plan to save some of what you earn, you need to ask the question, "How am I going to invest this money?" A good financial planner is important. Seek out someone who can give you good solid advice. My first financial adviser was my father. After some years, I hired a professional adviser. As you get into a career, ask how they are paid. It will help you secure the best financial adviser for your financial situation.

53

Learn how to study and teach yourself material. If you are taking a class in high school or college, often the teacher will explain how you will be tested. This is key to how to remember the information. Multiple-choice tests give you a chance at an answer; essay exams require you to compose the answer. I always told my students to study their material is short amounts of time: study for ten minutes, get up and walk around, study again for ten minutes, get up and walk around. The brain can remember more this way. Also, a quiet environment where you can speak the material out loud to yourself is a way to internalize information. If this is not possible, writing the information over and over also helps retention. Both recitation and writing slow down the brain and foster retention.

54

Learn how to tie a necktie and bow tie. You will be invited at some point in your life to a formal occasion where this may be the attire. You may not have anyone there to help you, so being able to dress yourself is part of preparing for many occasions that you will celebrate.

55

Learn how to sew on a button, fix a hem, and re-pair a zipper. Spending money on quick-fix repairs can add up. So can replacing items of clothing that need only small fixes. Being able to sew on a button and fix a zipper or hem can give longevity to these items of clothing.

56

Learn how to iron a shirt, a tablecloth, and a pair of pants. Learn how to do laundry and fold it properly. You will need to get ready for an interview and have properly ironed clothing. Your home will need things cleaned, ironed, and stored. When ironing a shirt, begin with the collar, then the sleeves, and finally the body of the shirt. Remember to not put a crease down the sleeve, but rather, iron to the fold and not on the fold and then move the fabric to reach all parts of it. Pants should be folded using the seams in the legs as guides. Put all the seams together, and then iron the creases down the front. If there are pockets, be sure to press the internal pocket as well.

57

earn how to use common household appliances: gas and electric stoves, toaster ovens, Crock-Pots, microwaves, coffeepots, dishwashers, and washers and dryers. If you go away to college, you will need to do laundry. If you move out of town, you will need to do laundry. It is just a part of life no matter where you are. Learn to sort clothes based on colors and fabrics for different temperatures.

58

Learn where the shutoff valves for water and electrical fuse or circuit breaker boxes are in any dwelling you live in. It is always good to know how to get the lights back on if a fuse or circuit breaker trips. For repairs that involve the plumbing in a home—replacing a faucet, fixing a drain, etc.—it is vital to know where to turn the water off. There is usually a nearby valve that can shut off the water to a particular sink, etc. as well as a shutoff valve for the entire dwelling.

59

Learn how to hang and properly clean trousers, shirts, and coats. Clothing can look better and last longer with good care. Some clothing must be dry-cleaned. I like to do my dry-cleaning at the store. If I see a tag that says dry-clean only, I think about how often it will need to be dry-cleaned. If it is something that needs that service each time I wear it, I would reconsider purchasing it; however, if it is an outer coat or garment, it may be reasonable. Items of clothing have laundering methods that are recommended. Follow those directions for best results. To avoid having to iron everything that comes out of the dryer, try to remove the items just before they are completely dry and hang them immediately. Hanging trousers/pants on proper hangers reduces wrinkles. Hanging shirts and coats properly by folding the collars and buttoning them keeps them looking better for future wearing.

6 0

Learn how to dial alphanumeric phone numbers. Some numbers are given with words and numbers, 1-800-IAM-COOL, for example. The letters are found with each number on the phone.

61

Learn how to tell time on both digital and analog clocks. We often see the time digitally: 2:30 p.m.; however, knowing how to tell time on a clock face with a small hand for minutes, big hand for hours, and second hand for seconds is also important.

62

Learn the planets in our solar system. There are nine (or eight) planets in our solar system. (In the late 1990s, astronomers began to argue whether Pluto should be called a planet due to its small size and position in the solar system.) Here's the list: Mercury, Venus, Earth, Mars, Jupiter, Saturn, Uranus, Neptune, and Pluto.

63

Learn how the American government works. Learn how a bill becomes law, what the branches of our government are, and how the president is elected. The president heads the Executive Branch. The president carries out the federal laws and recommends new ones, directs national defense and foreign policy, and performs ceremonial duties. The power of the president includes directing government, commanding the armed forces, and dealing with international powers. The president also acts as chief of law enforcement and holds the power to veto. The Legislative Branch is headed by Congress, which includes the Senate and the House of Representatives. These two bodies make laws. The power of this branch of government includes passing laws, originating spending bills, impeaching officials, and approving treaties. The Supreme Court heads the Judicial Branch. The powers of this branch include interpreting the Constitution, reviewing laws, and deciding cases involving states' rights.

64

Learn when to let go and walk away. There will be times in life when you need to take a totally different direction, either in relationships or in employment. Realize that taking a different path is often the best way to realize your goals.

65

Learn simple math and how to read a ruler and tape measure in metric units as well as in the US unit system. Learn how to measure volume in both systems, too. Learn to do addition in your head. This will be helpful when you are grocery shopping and need to think about the total cost of groceries before you get to the register, as well as in other everyday scenarios.

66

Learn how to convert temperature from Fahrenheit to Celsius and back again. The United States is one of the few countries that do not use Celsius or the metric system. Other countries, Canada for one, are aware of and relate to Fahrenheit, but do not use it traditionally. When traveling out of the country, it is wise to know how to pack and dress for certain temperatures, so knowing Celsius comes in handy.

67

Learn how to use a copy machine, a telephone with multiple lines, a calculator, and a fax machine. Upon employment, spend your "training time" for your new job with more important things. Find out how to use a type of each of these office machines and then adapt by taking your knowledge of them and learning the version at your workplace.

L earn Roman numerals.

$$I = 1$$
$$V = 5$$
$$X = 10$$
$$L = 50$$
$$C = 100$$
$$D = 500$$
$$M = 1,000$$

Placing a letter before or after another letter indicates subtraction from or addition to the letter, respectively. For example, XL = 40 (50 – 10); LX = 60 (50 + 10).

69

L earn how many pennies are in a nickel, how many nickels are in a dime, etc. There are five pennies in a nickel, two nickels in a dime, two dimes and one nickel in a quarter, and four quarters in a dollar. If returning change to a person, count it back to the amount given to make change. For example, if something costs $14.59 and a person gives you $20, count back this way: 41 cents makes $15, and $5 makes 20.

70

Learn the currencies of major countries and know how a rate of exchange works. Each country has its own currency that has value on a global level. Some currencies are strong and some are weak, based on a world economy. The most important knowledge to have is the quantity of that currency you receive for each US dollar you exchange and compare that to what you can purchase with that amount. A simple example is if you get 1.5 Euros for one dollar. In the United States you can purchase a beverage for one dollar, and in the European Union you can purchase the beverage for 1.5 Euros; the exchange is equal. However, if it costs three Euros for the same item, the foreign currency is weaker. The purchasing power of the foreign currency value based on the US dollar is what determines the weakness or strength of a currency.

Learn how to hail a taxi. In some larger cities, a good way to get from point A to point B is by taxi. In some cities, like New York City, traveling by taxi is preferred to owning a car. Raising your hand when you see that a taxi is free signals the taxi to approach you. The light will be illuminated on top when the taxi is in service.

72

L earn the tenets of major and minor religions of the world and the special qualities associated with each. As an adult, you will meet many new people from different walks of life and places. Learn to ask about their belief systems and customs politely. "Would you please explain how you celebrate your major holidays?" "I am interested in knowing why you wear a certain type of clothing." "I would be very interested in hearing about your dietary laws." One's religion, as is one's politics, is at the soul of his or her character. Showing interest in others' belief systems shows that you care about them. It was once the rule that one should not talk about religion or politics in social settings. However, in an academically motivated social conversation, polite questions and responses to those topics provide a lively discussion.

73

Learn the months of the year and which seasons are associated with which months. Also learn the major religious and national holidays and when they occur in the year. Winter includes the latter part of December and continues through January, February, and most of March. Spring includes the latter part of March and continues through April, May, and most of June. Summer begins in the latter part of June and continues through July, August, and most of September. Fall begins in the latter part of September and continues through October, November, and most of December.

74

Learn the difference between Washington, DC, and Washington State; Austria and Australia; Sweden and Switzerland; and Greenland and Iceland.

75

Learn how to read a street map. GPS systems are popular, but you may be the one creating them someday! Learn how to utilize maps without the use of a technological device. Taking a vacation into areas where there is no Internet reception for map applications allows you to get involved with a field map and find your way. It's not a bad idea to learn to use a compass for an adventure like this, too. Reading a topographical map is important to see the terrain of an area.

76

Learn the differences between a nationality and a place of origin and between ethnicity and culture. Your place of origin is where you were born. Your nationality is where you legally reside. Your ethnicity is your common ancestral, social, cultural, or national experience. The culture of a people is the common customs, arts, social achievements, and social institutions.

77

Learn the names of languages and which countries speak them. Know some common phrases in several languages, especially if you plan to travel to areas where they are spoken. Know some Latin.

Guten Morgen, Buenos dias, Bonjour, Buongiorno ("Good morning" or "Good day" in German, Spanish, French, and Italian)

78

Learn how to rent a car. For example, at what age is it legal to do so, and how do insurances and licenses transfer to rental cars here and abroad?

79

Learn at what temperature water boils and freezes. Know the safe temperatures to store and eat foods. Know that food temperature is important for safe storage and consuming of food both in your dorm room and in your home.

80

Learn the words to the "The Star Spangled Banner" and the Pledge of Allegiance to the US flag. Stand and place your hand over your heart for the pledge unless you have a religious conflict. Remove your hat when saying the pledge and singing the national anthem.

81

Along with basic government and how it works, learn how you can change or initiate a law or an ordinance within your city or town. Learn how to vote in local elections. Know where to apply for a voter's registration and where to vote in local government and national elections.

82

Learn how to mow a lawn, plant a tree, and tend to property you may own. Home ownership will include outdoor maintenance. Learning basic landscaping skills will help reduce expenses. Good "curb appeal" also increases the market value of your home.

83

Learn how to polish your shoes. Nicely polished and well-maintained shoes are part of the whole package of dressing for success.

84

Learn basic bicycle maintenance. Learn how to change a tire and add air to it and how to fix a chain. Keeping a little tool kit on board is a good idea.

85

Learn how to build a fire and put it out. In your fireplace, fire pit, barbecue grill, or campsite, learn how to safely start and tend a fire with wood or charcoal. Learn how to extinguish it.

86

Learn how to pitch a tent and be safe in the outdoors. Sporting goods stores and guidebooks often have classes or lessons on survival skills in the outdoors. If you are an adventure traveler, it is wise to be equipped with this skill. Learn how to pack for outdoor travel, find and cook food, and find or build a shelter.

Learn how to dust, vacuum, make a bed, and scrub a floor, toilet, and sink. Everyone needs to learn basic housekeeping chores. These chores are part of daily and weekly living. Keeping a home tidy on a weekly basis is part of life.

88

Learn how to knit or do some type of craft. **Know how to draw basic shapes.** Not everyone is "crafty," but being interested in something that uses the right side of your brain is important. In clubs and other groups, at after-work events, and at neighborhood gatherings, a skill in some craft will be a handy tool.

Learn to develop many hobbies. You will not work your entire life, hopefully, so you will need to fill your free time with things you like to do.

L **earn the difference between a synonym, antonym, and homonym.** A synonym is a word that shares the basic meaning of another word (saunter/walk/stroll). An antonym is a word that has the opposite meaning of another word (difficult/easy). A homonym is a word that sounds like another word but has different meanings (daze/days).

Learn what a simile and a metaphor are and how to use each one correctly. A simile is when two unlike things are compared with the words "like" or "as." (He is as hungry as a horse.) A metaphor is using a phrase to compare two unlike objects. (His dependable brother is his rock.)

92

Learn how to receive and follow verbal and written directions. You should be able to listen to verbal directions and remember all the steps. Following written directions, such as directions to a location, steps in a recipe, or instructions in a manual to assemble something, is important for a good outcome.

93

Learn to take responsibility for your actions and put other people before yourself. Learn to serve others and treat them the way you'd want to be treated. This age-old axiom is still one of the best recommendations for life!

94

earn how to efficiently and effectively wash a car and change the oil (even if you never have to). Also learn how to check the tires' air pressure and add air if needed, and learn how to change a tire.

95

Learn the uses and meanings of particular titles given to people: Mr., Mrs., Ms., Sir, Esquire, Your Excellence, Your Honor, Madam Secretary, Mr. President, Madam Chairperson.

96

Learn basic knowledge of computer programs beyond gaming, Internet, and social media applications. Learn how to create a spreadsheet, create a word-processing document, and how to use a photo-storage program. You will need these in your personal life, and they may be needed in your work environment.

97

Learn some basic home repairs. Learn how to clean out a drain, clean the showerhead, fix a squeaky door hinge, hang a picture, repair scuffed flooring (linoleum or hardwood). Learn how to remove decals from surfaces; polish silver, brass, and copper; fix stuck sliding windows; and untangle extension cords. **Learn how to do some basic electrical work.** Learn how to change a light bulb (especially one that is stuck), repair a switch, fix a lamp, and replace a fuse or reset a circuit breaker. Know where the fuse box or circuit breaker panel is located in your dwelling.

98

Learn to understand the impact your job or life-style has on the world: global, economic, and social. Reading about the company you work for and how its services or products reach out into the world is important knowledge for you as an employee as well as a citizen.

99

Learn to have patience, a sense of humor, and, most of all, a sense of wonder.

Made in the USA
Columbia, SC
17 December 2019